JOSH ALLEN

GET A JOB! IF YOU WANT TO BE POOR FOREVER

SAVE YOUR KIDS FROM THE SCHOOL-TO-JOB DEBT SENTENCE

First published by 22 E Square Ltd 2024

Copyright © 2024 by Josh Allen

All rights reserved. No part of this publication may be reproduced, stored or transmitted in any form or by any means, electronic, mechanical, photocopying, recording, scanning, or otherwise without written permission from the publisher. It is illegal to copy this book, post it to a website, or distribute it by any other means without permission.

Josh Allen asserts the moral right to be identified as the author of this work.

Josh Allen has no responsibility for the persistence or accuracy of URLs for external or third-party Internet Websites referred to in this publication and does not guarantee that any content on such Websites is, or will remain, accurate or appropriate.

Designations used by companies to distinguish their products are often claimed as trademarks. All brand names and product names used in this book and on its cover are trade names, service marks, trademarks and registered trademarks of their respective owners. The publishers and the book are not associated with any product or vendor mentioned in this book. None of the companies referenced within the book have endorsed the book.

First edition

This book was professionally typeset on Reedsy.
Find out more at reedsy.com

As a man thinketh, so is he.

> PROVERBS 23:7
> THE HOLY BIBLE

Contents

Acknowledgement		ii
1	Introduction	1
2	What's This Book About?	3
3	Work To Live. Don't Live To Work	7
4	Get To The Point (everything is being done so that you get...	10
5	Choose	12
6	Prison? How? How It's A Trap And A Prison	13
7	How There's No Escape For Most	18
8	Steer Your Kids to Freedom	20
9	How To Start	23
10	CONCLUSION	32
11	RESOURCES	35

Acknowledgement

"Yes, I am the vine; you are the branches. Those who remain in me, and I in them, will produce much fruit. For apart from me you can do nothing."

   -The King of kings, Jesus Christ.

Apart from Him, I can do nothing. Blessed is His Name forever and ever.

   Thank you, my Lord for all that you have done for me. Any good that comes from this book is due to Him. Glorify Him every soul. This life is but a vapor. His Kingdom is forever. Give your life to Him.

1

Introduction

You will accept this or reject this. Either way, it is sincerely written. With any new information, there are generally two responses; to agree or to disagree; to accept it, or to reject it. It's like that scene from the 1999 film *The Matrix*. Spoiler alert: You might respond like Neo, and initially buck and kick, but eventually embrace and then thrive. Or, you might respond like Cypher, and forever reject it in your spirit, and wish it were that you never knew. "Ignorance is bliss." Cue the harp. But is it, though?

The whole point of this is that I have learned, the very, very hard way, that ignorance is in fact, slavery, or as the title says, prison. At least in the matters of financial literacy. It's an invisible prison. You and I are quite literally serving time; life in fact. You have no walls (some of the time), but you cannot escape its confines. You go where it tells you to go, you do what it tells you to do, and you do so when you are told to.

This is where we split the population into two; those who accept this fact, or those who don't. We, most of us, live in this constant discomfort of this prison, but for some, it has the comfort of familiarity. It's all they've ever known. So no matter how uncomfortable, no matter how painful, they would rather stay here. The other side is too uncertain. Too scary. Prison for myself and my children and my children's children is the devil I know. But at least I know him. This book is MY opinion as well as my interpretation of some facts. I promised myself that I would share knowledge on how to help others if I ever got it. I believe this information will be helpful to others.

I am not sure that I can convince you otherwise if you are one of these. However, if you are one of the ones that feel, deep in your bones, that this is NOT how life is supposed to be, not in 2024 or our general contemporary time period - that there's gotta be more to life than this - that you have been vaguely, or acutely aware of the fact that you are not free - that it HAS to be possible to escape it, then my friend, you are the one that this book is written for. You are the Neo of your family and its future generations.

I want it to be a very, very brief overview, just to inject hope in you, because this subject can go deep. Very deep. But, I want to provide, perhaps, a starting point. Perhaps if you've been on this quest for some time already. I want to provide some sort of outline to organize the information and then organize the plan.

I'm organizing the plan as I write. But, I want to first provide an overview, and then with subsequent books, Lord willing, to detail each aspect so that you can choose one or more of those paths to free yourself and your family.

Overview first, to organize the chaos. Outline to show you what the problem is and how we are indeed in a prison that keeps us in chains all of our lives. Then lastly, an outline on how we escape it.

2

What's This Book About?

OK, enough with the vague generalities.

This book says this: we live to work and then die, more than likely in debt, and then continue this cycle with our kids. Like I said, this can go deep. So, I will do my best and we will keep it fairly superficial. But what I want you to take away is that THERE IS AN ESCAPE.

What This Book Is Not Saying

What this book is not saying is to NOT get a job, or to work. Besides the sense of value to oneself that a job might bring, our society would fall apart, and you and your family would starve if you didn't.

We need roads, engineers, bridges, buildings, a power grid (maybe), medical practitioners, and plumbers. We need services like accounting, financial advice, and legal advice.

These are all jobs. We need them.

Why Say What I'm Saying?

We end up in the above and many other jobs as part of a machine. If, like the 1950s U.S.A., having one of these jobs allowed you to care for your family, buy them a house, have vacations, and then retire comfortably, then I would not be saying a job is a prison, or part of a prison.

We are not in those times anymore. Our reality is this: you are born. You are free and happy, in blissful ignorance, until around age four. That's when you enter the pipeline of careful indoctrination to become a drone that will play its part with little to no fuss, until it is too old and worn out to be of use, and then put out to pasture. And then die.

In that process, your knowledge, WAY OF THINKING, that is, your *mindset*, outlook, dreams, hopes, and imagination and behavior are carefully curated so that you enter the workforce in your "chosen" role. Soon after which you are trapped into said role, or another, just to keep up with never ending, ever-increasing financial demands. You most likely do this while stumbling around in the dark until you get to what is supposed to be retirement. Alas, you can't stop working. Your body is sick from aging, you have been working for about forty years at this point, and you either have nothing to show for it, or you have things, but you are in debt. If you stop paying for them, they all go away. You end up sleeping on a grate or having to live with your adult children or other relatives because you simply cannot support yourself. Guess what, they can barely support you because they are on the same track that you are on, only just a few decades behind you.

In the meantime, throughout that whole time, somebody, you don't know who, was making money off of you at every turn. And I mean EVERY single turn. When you finally pass, your family will be in great shock to learn of a whole new layer of costs and expenses that came with the mere and inevitable fact of your death.

So, you've spent your main years on this earth struggling, barely able to make ends meet. If you took vacations, it was likely on credit. You don't have any significant wealth to pass onto your kids so that it might be easier on them. Not only do you not have any monetary wealth to

WHAT'S THIS BOOK ABOUT?

pass onto them, you don't even have any valuable INFORMATION that they might use to steer away from the path that they are on, which brought you to where you are. The cycle continues.

This is the 95% or more of us. I have lived this life. Even after coming to this realization, I realized that even if I had become AWARE of our prison, the walls were too high. I couldn't climb out. I couldn't find a way out. Maybe it was better to just be vaguely aware that I was a prisoner. But to know, and not be able to get out…well, that's another dimension of despair.

THIS book that you are currently reading IS that INFORMATION. But, more than mere information, it is a manual of sorts.

This manual starts with this idea:

There are three layers to become free. It is possible.

1. The mind
2. The information
3. The actions/behavior

They, whoever "they" are, have played a number on the collective's mind. Information abounds in our current age, but like cells which can't absorb sugar to give the body the energy that it needs to survive (because they can't produce insulin - because insulin brings the sugar into the cell) our minds can't absorb all this information. Our minds have been made impervious to this useful and vital way of thinking, that is, to the mindset.

The mind needs to be revamped to be able to absorb and accept and ultimately USE that information to become free.

This books aims to:

1. Make you aware of all this
2. Show you that the mind CAN be taught to change in order to;
3. Seek out and absorb the knowledge
4. Start you on the direction using steps on how to think of things, and what to perhaps aim for in order to start building your escape
5. Start to guide your children into a direction that will ensure that their years of labor are not pointless; rather, that they labor to build comfort and security for themselves and their own families, and ultimately communities

In other words, this book aims to guide you to:

<u>FREEDOM</u>

3

Work To Live. Don't Live To Work

In my financial services business, one of the very first things that we get clients to do is to stop for a minute or two and dream. Nothing fancy, just your top five list of financial goals and then the question, "If money were of no concern, what would you do?"

It is shocking how many people seem to be thinking of this for the very first time. They are taken aback, and they genuinely seem to have no idea. Why? Because they have never really imagined that "money could be no issue." They tend to generally give answers like, "I would travel more." OK, that's a start.

But this shows that for most people, they live to work. They don't just work in order to be able to live. They literally live JUST for work. Other things like family, rest and relaxation, their true purpose in life, serving others in meaningful ways MUST find some space around that work. Yet for most, they are not in some dream job - one that fulfills some greater purpose in them than just living expenses. From Sunday night on, there's the dread of Monday morning. Monday morning is an absolute drag, so much so that we've given it nicknames; The Mondays, Manic Monday, Monday Blues…

Tuesday is us settling into acceptance of the week. Friday is still yet far away. Wednesday lifts up our spirits a bit. It's Hump day, after all, because we're crossing over the halfway mark through the work week. Thursday has a bit more morale, because it's almost Friday. And then finally, at long last, it's Friday, Fri-yay, TGIF (Thank Goodness It's Friday)! I've liked quite a few songs that celebrated this fact over the years. Somehow, we're able to slip away before the day is even done on a Friday. I guess even the bosses understand. And this is only SOME jobs.

The lineups at the liquor store are long. The clubs have long lineups as well on both Friday and Saturday nights. Sunday morning is spent dreading that the weekend is coming to an end. Who ever decided that the weekend should be only two days anyway?! That's why the occasional Long weekend is so uplifting.

And for each of those inspiring work days it looks something like this: you wake up very early and get the kids ready for school (your future replacements at your job). You have a crowded commute either on the road with other drivers like yourself, in the dark during winters, or packed like sardines in some bus or train, where you see everybody's blank face, some getting a little bit of extra sleep, while others read books, magazines, or newspapers, and others still just stare blankly into nothingness. At work you clock in, get your second coffee, chit chat and get to it. Greetings include phrases like, "Five more days to the weekend!" The countdown to lunch or even the first break has begun. Lunch is a reprieve. Smokers get their mini escapes during smoke breaks. After lunch the first hour is OK, but two or three hours in, there's a crash. The countdown to the end of the day continues. Finally, the end of day. Time to clock out. Time for that commute again. For some, it's an hour or more. Hours which amount to literal years over a work lifetime. YEARS of your life, just sitting in traffic.

What's all this for? Well, because a mortgage is waiting for you. Did you know that the literal meaning of that word is "death pledge?"

If not a mortgage, then it's the rent. Rent is money that you are pouring into a hole (because it is gone forever) while trying to save up or get your credit good enough to be able to get a mortgage. A phone bill or five are waiting for you, because well, everybody just has to have a phone. There must be power and water in that house or apartment. Those bills are waiting for you too. Everyone in your house eats, and not just for nourishment. They eat snacks, they eat because they're bored, they eat and eat and eat. They need clothes and school demands, extracurricular activities. There's car payments, insurances, maintenance, debt.

Oftentimes, these expenses (the realities of life) happen to you sort of gradually. One day you're working, or going to school, with some of these expenses yes, but you still feel relatively free. Maybe you live at home with your parents, or maybe you're just young, single, and carefree. You meet someone and intentionally or not, you're together. One more person to take into account in all your expenses. Before long, a baby comes along. Now, that job that you just had for fun is a must-have. If not this one, it must be another. Now, you are at the mercy of the moods, character, or personality of your supervisor(s), colleagues, and ultimately your employer. Much must now be compromised for the sake of your very survival. Yours and that of your loved ones.

Over the years, this just becomes an accepted reality. The cost of living rises eternally. You now live to work. You have no choice. Like I said, this is an overview of the situation. Without getting much deeper into this portion of the subject, I hope that I'm making my point. You are not having a life, where you go and work, get commensurate remuneration, and then use it to actually live out a purpose, secure retirement, grow enough to pass onto your kids, and then retire, or just stop HAVING to work to survive.

You live to work. For all the years of your life that you are capable, you LIVE TO WORK.

4

Get To The Point (everything is being done so that you get to the point)

So, people may not have ready answers to the question, "What would you do if money were no factor," but deep down, and not THAT deep down, everybody wants a life. They want a life where they don't feel trapped and strangled; by having no savings, mounting debt, and nothing to leave their children.

Everybody wants to work, so that they can live, but with plenty of living still available. They want that thing, or at least the time and opportunity to seek out and find that thing that was a glimmer in their eye as children, "When I grow up…." They want to do the work that they have to do so that they can get TO THE POINT. Whatever the point of their own life is. Imagine if money wasn't stopping you, the adventure that it would be to either be living your purpose, or spending the time trying to find it, knowing that you have a home, with its utilities covered, with all the basic necessities of your family covered.

I imagine working then, while at work would see you put in a little bit more, maybe a lot more effort. Morale would be higher. Maybe days and months wouldn't be spent literally counting down to your death (Yes, it's a morbid view. But living a life wherein day after day is spent counting down to the next day, and then the next Friday, week after week, month after month, year after year is a LITERAL countdown to your death). Imagine that, having spent the bulk of those "when I grow up" years counting down to your own end. In between those work weeks (or days), you spent the time self-medicated, or numbed with alcohol and whatever else, as well as mindless entertainment from the idiot box.

I'm deliberately being a little condescending here; but my beef is not with you, the one blindly ushered into this invisible prison, but it is with whoever made it so. It bothers me very much that a world of souls with so much to give has been masterfully turned into imprisoned drones and then kept too busy to see it, or even do anything about it if they do.

You know, maybe if 100% of us were drones, and we didn't see real people actually living their lives, seemingly outside of this prison, then maybe I would not even see it myself. Maybe the dream of freedom would just be some vague concept in the back of my mind while I slave away in my cubicle or assembly line or oil rig or hospital ward; you get the picture. But we do see them. The 5%. There are those who are not in this trap.

What this book aims to do: I want to show you that it is possible to either be one of these free ones, or to start your children on that journey so that is they aren't just your replacement in the hamster wheel of life, but that they can end up in a much better position and then ultimately break the cycle for your successive generations.

I want to open your eyes, and then start you on the way to freedom. Maybe you'll get there in this lifetime. Or maybe you'll do it just so your kids don't live as despairing an outlook.

5

Choose

Choose The Job/Career Route With Full Awareness

As has already been mentioned, what this book is not saying is that jobs aren't important. In fact, they are vital for the functioning and survival of any society. However, there's a subtle way in which the focus and direction and reason for jobs has changed over time. I don't know if this was always the ultimate goal, but that's not really relevant for our discussion here. The point is, now, jobs aren't what they are supposed to be. So, if you choose a job, and guide your children towards the mindset and the life of having a job, I want you to do it with some awareness.

I suspect that the ones with whom this book resonates want that awareness so that they can do something about it.

6

Prison? How? How It's A Trap And A Prison

We've touched on the present realities of living a life with a job. I don't think that surprises anyone. I just described your life, most of you! The average person is of average intelligence. So how indeed, can a whole society, a whole world almost, be duped into voluntary slavery or prison? Again, remember that this is the story of The Matrix, of sorts. Either you are open to new information, or you are not. But I'll wager that the reason that there are only 5% (or less) who are free in this world is because the majority are firmly under the Dunning-Kruger effect; too proud and too self-assured in their ignorance (lack of knowledge) to see that they don't have enough knowledge, and thereby would not to go to seek it out in order to improve their situation. As a result, they remain where they are. They are too stupid to understand that they are too stupid. I'm sorry. I have to shock and offend a little bit to drive the point.

Do you know the anecdote of the frog and the boiling water? A frog that is thrown into a pot of boiling water immediately jumps out. The danger is clear and immediately apparent. But place a frog in a pot of room-temperature water, and the frog will relax. Place that pot on the stove and slowly turn up the heat. That frog will slowly boil to death and not leave! That's the story anyway. I can't say I've tried to observe this personally. But the story still illustrates a real life principle nevertheless. When the acclimatization is slow and gradual, the change may never be noticed, even if it kills you in the end!

In our society this water is, well, society. It is the most impactful and major aspect of it. I have boiled it down to four main components: media (television, movies, magazines, social media), school, community (family and surroundings), and the government. All around you, the message comes that to take your rightful place in society, you must go to school (and the government will intervene if this isn't done).

Your television is filled with pointless entertainment that mostly shows how humans relate to one another. Directly or indirectly it tells you what is the right way to be and what is the wrong way to be in society. When you watch a television show, they provide you with a few templates of acceptable characters. Choose which one you either already fit into, or would like to become. But there are also the templates of the unacceptable types, the black sheep.

Reality, talk, and morning shows have these "ideal" representatives that tell you what is and what isn't acceptable. You are herded into "correct" behavior with the fear of not fitting in. Because the majority of people, including your potential friends, romantic partners, employers, and colleagues are all in this group, you MUST find your way to fit into the group. Unacceptable views or ways of being are usually pointed out by the group, usually led by these representatives (show hosts or new anchors or main characters of TV shows), by CONDESCENSION. That seems to be the biggest weapon.

Either explicitly or implicitly, your news, show, or commercial will present a position as the correct and acceptable position, as if it's the most obvious thing in the world. Most of the aforementioned group (your potential friends, boyfriend and girlfriends, employers etc) accept and assimilate that directive as if it's the "most obvious thing in the world" as well, and then they propagate the same message at the appropriate time to others.

Woe to those who question ANYTHING that the main group says or believes.

School will gently guide you over a minimum of thirteen years, with mostly inconsequential knowledge and systems of herding you and teaching you to conform to your peers at the threat of not being accepted by said peers. You spend your most malleable years learning to sit quietly, learning by regurgitating information that is largely utterly useless for the real life that you will have to live when you come out of the school system and into the workforce.

You don't learn. Not really. You learn to memorize random information. Your success is measured by how much you can re-state that information in a quiz or test. You get mental exercises in the form of math. Unless you are going to be a physicist, engineer, scientist, or mathematician, most of it is utterly useless past grade six or so.

In recent years, school subjects have become even more irrelevant to regular life. Much time is spent on made-up concepts and abstract social ideas. It is inconceivable how entirely subjective subjects have pass-or-fail standards.

In the group are also your family and neighbors. So, from the cradle, they are teaching you and guiding you along the same lines, because THEY themselves must live within those lines. Can you blame them? They want what is best for their precious child. "Don't make waves. Just conform and survive. Live a life of "success" by the prescribed standards for the envy of others if you can." "Don't be weird" is essentially the message. So, they'll have you in play groups, kindergarten, school, and then off to the final and the worst stage of the school system: post-secondary, to finalize your indoctrination. Unless the particular post-secondary institution sticks only to the relevant subjects of the main field of study like engineering, law, science etc, then there is no exception in my statement. I mean that even those who go to study something specific like building bridges, for instance, must include some indoctrination-style subjects in order to graduate. So that even they are not excluded from the statement that post-secondary for them is the final stage of indoctrination, at least as far as academia is concerned.

Media and community continue, academia is for a time, but the government presides over them all. It is the enforcement arm of it all. As we recently saw around the world - just in case you thought you lived in a free country - governments rule over your life. You may have thought you were free to believe and act as you wish, within the confines of a constitution, but it should be apparent now that this is not the case.

Part of what maintains the effective prison of the job-state of your and most of our lives is taxation. You are effectively under tax-slavery. This is part of what forces you to be in and to remain in the hamster wheel job-prison. You are taxed at every turn. You are taxed when you earn, when you buy, when you sell, when you invest, when you profit, when you buy a property, when you continue to live on the property, when you pass on your hard-earned wealth to your children, and then after you die.

Say you awaken to the uselessness - useless to you, but not to them, because school accomplished its goal of creating the perfect tax-paying, unquestioning, obedient citizen - and decide that you want to pull your child out of the drone-factory that is the traditional school system. Overlord government will be knocking on your door fairly soon, inquiring as to why your child isn't at the indoctrination camp. Pardon me, I mean school.

It gets so much worse. But, as this book is an overview, I won't get into too many more examples. Like I said, I probably can't change your mind if you already believe otherwise. But if you already had a sense of this, then all this makes sense to you. It may seem like I'm rambling, but there's a point. I'm demonstrating how indeed it is that we live in a prison-complex if we live the life of a regular job, and how we end up there.

Regardless of whether you are with me or not on this point about government, you surely must see that the government has a say in almost every aspect of your life; down to your thoughts; literally thought-crimes as imagined by Orwell.

Right now, you may be in alignment with whatever the government prescribes. The true measure, if you really want to see how much of a lack of freedom we now have, is to imagine, under the same standards, that now YOU are in a position that is contrary to the government.

7

How There's No Escape For Most

As demonstrated thus far, you should be able to see how extensive the prison that outwardly manifests as the job or rat race actually is. Its roots are in the mind. Its infrastructure is mostly invisible. But the end-result is the same: financially trapped with no conceivable hope of escape.

The escape seems impossible because the main chains are in the mind. It is the mind that you need in order to think of the solution to it, and devise an escape. But if the mind that you are equipped with is itself the prison - or its anchor, then it would seem inescapable.

Not only is it firmly anchored and deep, it consists of being buttressed by personalities which are given to it, personalities of the type that can never escape because they have pride, arrogance, cowardice. Whoa whoa, is it ever a good idea to insult your audience?

I'm not trying to insult you. I'm trying to shake you out of it. Harriet Tubman was a former slave during American slavery, who, after she had found freedom, would go back again and again to try to free others. She is quoted as saying, "I could have freed so many more, if only I could convince them that they were slaves." There are now claims that she never said this. Fine. Whether she said it or not, the point still stands. It illustrates my point perfectly. This comes in part from human nature. I guess whoever designed this prison took that part into account; human hubris as part of the very structure that would hold up the prison. People like to think that they are smarter than they are. No one likes to say, "Oh, I didn't know that," or "I was wrong" or "Teach me this thing that is completely outside my worldview." No one likes to feel duped, or admit that they have been tricked.

However, in order to become free of this prison, one must be free of this arrogance. One must become humble enough to learn from the very bottom up. You must be willing to learn 1+1 again. This is the beginning of your freedom.

8

Steer Your Kids to Freedom

What to teach them

Ok. So, what should you do for the next generations? Say you are not able or willing to home-school or alternative-school them, then begin guiding them in a few ways.

Guide Their Thinking

Guide their thinking. GIGO stands for Garbage In, Garbage Out. Start to limit the amount of time that they spend in front of screens. Any screens. Start to consider the kinds of things that are on your TV. A big step would be getting rid of live television altogether. With streaming services, it's some steps better, simply because some thought has to go into what will be watched. None of this will happen quickly. It probably shouldn't. Rather, with some sense of urgency, it should be done somewhat gently. Some things will have to be banned altogether if I had my way. Not really, because I believe in freedom. Perhaps not banned on a societal level, but I think each in his household can make that executive decision. I would ban Reality television.

The news is definitely to be avoided at all costs - that is one of the worst poisons on television. Just as bad, are the celebrity worship shows that tend to follow the 6:00 news. That is truly a waste of life, mind, and soul.

I will reiterate that this book is an overview. So, we won't get into all the whys and hows, but trust me. It is brain rot for you and your children.

One of the main allures of these things on TV is that they are distractions. They help you to take your mind off the prison in which you live by completely setting your focus on something which has absolutely NO benefit, but instead is actually detrimental to you. Your emotions are engaged and manipulated. You go to bed. You have something to discuss around the water-cooler or break room, or read and understand in the next day's gossip column, or watch being discussed by your favorite YouTuber or TikToker.

But, YEARS pass by and your life has no significant improvement from any of this. I remember awakening to this after years of daytime television. Maury, Ricky, Jenny, Jerry, the Everest commercials, then soaps, then the judge shows. It's a pointless cycle to keep your mind numb.

Be engaged about what they are learning in school. Ask them everyday. Respond to and go to parent teacher meetings. Challenge the teachers on what they are being taught.

But, it must all start with you. Begin to read or watch personal development information. I don't subscribe to the magical hooey about laws of attraction and things of that nature. But there is a great deal of value in exposing yourself to information about thinking differently, adopting positive habits into one's life, and how successful people think. Again, although a bunch of them preach it, stay away from any spiritual aspects of that.

I will insert my personal beliefs here: If it's not proclaiming Christ Jesus in accordance with the Holy Bible (because many will "mix" Jesus with "other."), then it is not the spiritual self-development that you need.

Engaging your mind in these things will be like the prisoner who has begun to spend time looking out the window out into the meadow, after years of not even being aware that their cell had a window. You will start to dream; to have hope.

9

How To Start

I recommend starting with the book by Robert Kiyosaki: Rich Dad, Poor Dad: What The Rich Teach Their Kids About Money That The Poor and The Middle Class Do Not. Read it or listen to it, and then get your kids to do the same, over and over again.

First, you must see the game, and then learn how to win it. Most of us are in the game and are completely unaware of it. We feel the dreariness - the drudgery, and maybe the feeling of being trapped, but have no idea of the true structure of the game. So, start by becoming aware of the rules, and then for lack of a better word, start to reprogram yourself and your children.

The Meat

Remember, this is an overview. So, this will be very general.

The Employee trades his time for money. In my illustration so far in this book, this is the prisoner.

There are only so many hours in the day. Whether on wage or salary, the employee is limited in how much money he can make. Based on the conversations around the employee since he can remember, and then his own conversations when he's old enough, there are certain ranges of pay that are considered lousy, ok, pretty good, or really good.

The lawyer, for example, who might make $200-$500/hr might sound really good to the average employee. I'm not sure there are many who make that kind of money.

But, they have to do a LOT of work, after YEARS of EXPENSIVE schooling. That amount is limited and can only go up by so much.

On average an employee gets taxed about 40% of their pay and it only goes up from there with the money they make.

So, while that $500/hr sounds amazing, that's only on paper. That lawyer's real money is just about $200-$300/hr. How is that ok? About half of your time and life's work is just GONE. In other words, for about 40% of your week, month, or year, you work for FREE.

Then, when you go to buy ANYTHING with that money, it is all taxed again.

If you go and save some of that money, if you put it in an RRSP, 401(k),Super, SIPP (or your country's equivalent), you will likely get taxed again. If it gains any growth while being invested, that growth will get taxed. You get the picture.

That was our lawyer, who maybe feels maybe about how $500/hr looks on paper and is pacified by that, even though they aren't really HAVING $500/hr actually going into their bank account.

What about a more average pay of about $28-$38/hr? All the above still applies. Yet, with far less money.

What about the low wage earner with about $15/hr? Yet, all the same still applies to them as well?

The employee usually has hard work to do. By the time the day or week is over, they are done. They neither have the strength nor the will to think about much else. Yes, they can dream about improving their station in life, but thanks to the conditioning, all they've been taught is simply getting a "better job." This is just another part of the maze. All the same rules apply.

HOW TO START

It's an illusion. The job will hardly afford you a retirement, decent savings, or even legacy money to leave to your kids.

While your entire time was taken up by your labor, you didn't have the time or energy to learn what was outside the box. You didn't learn about essential things like life insurance (a good lump sum of money that your family can receive in the event of your death), which can usually be afforded for a modest amount; probably less than whatever you end up spending at your favorite takeout spot, or two or monthly subscriptions to your streaming services.

You didn't have time to learn about the very basics of the terrible mechanisms that are triggered when you die. Things like funeral costs, wills, estate fees, estate taxes, probate. I forget, is this just for the unlucky few, or does everybody die? I forget. Please remind me. Did you learn any of this in school? Or is Sin Cos of 30 earning you 'stack bundles' as the kids say; that is, fire-your-boss money?

Do you begin to see it now?

Free Yourself

Mindset

The mindset begins with GIGO. Take positive control of what goes into you. IT MATTERS. It's what created the current prisoner that is the present version of you. But, this book is about hope. Your current version does not have to be your forever version. Many, many have done it. You just have to decide. With concerted effort, people have made this transformation from one year, two, or even five years. It doesn't matter if it takes longer. Believe me, once your mind begins to be free, you start to become free, even if you are still in your job-prison. You have hope. You see a way out. You have started tunneling out, even if it's with a spoon. Five or ten years of tunneling means one day, you will be out. Doing nothing means you will NEVER be out, and neither will your kids, or their kids. The life of stress that you live now will be their lot and their legacy. So start.

Accumulate Assets

The foremost idea that should be at the back of your mind regarding money is this: my money should work for me as soon as possible! I will work for money until it does. This is where what I said at the beginning applies: you still have a job.

Look, whether you are one of the many who, if given a chance, would fire their boss, or you are one of the few that say, "I love my job and I would do it even if I won the lottery," this message is for all.

Work to live and don't live to work. The world needs you. Your children want more time with you while they're still young. Your spouse needs more quality time with you and they might appreciate being rescued from HAVING to work, even if they might still want to go to the job.

How you get your money to work for you is by acquiring ASSETS. Assets are not what your bank and the same system that taught you to be a slave says are. Assets are things that make you money. Whatever it costs to have them is less than what they make you. So, your house is NOT an asset, unless it brings in more money than it takes. Don't get offended. Get on the other side; the side that receives the money.

So, even if you want to keep your job, get your mind on getting assets. Many people rent out part of their home, so that it starts to pay them. The more money you have, the more money you can put into assets, or the bigger or better the assets you can get; which means they pay you more.

Dividend stocks are assets, but they are risky. They pay you money every month or quarter (third month). It depends on the company.

You can buy a house or building that will make you income from the rent that people pay. Another way is using the same house for Short-Term Rentals like AirBnB, VRBO etc.

HOW TO START

You can rent out cars, bikes, or something else. There seems to be an app for renting just about everything.

There are more pricey insurance policies that will pay you dividends, but also accumulate a pool of money that you can borrow from instead of borrowing from the bank. When you repay, you are repaying yourself. So, you use your money when you need it, but you get to get it back with the repayments. You need no hoops to jump through to qualify for that loan to yourself. The actual money is from the insurance company. You just borrow AGAINST the pool that IS your own money. That means YOUR pool of money continues to grow with *compound interest* (interest earning interest due to the amount of time that the money is sitting in that pool) uninterrupted. All the while, you still have life insurance, ie, the lump sum of money that will go to our family upon your passing, which is there the whole time.

You can buy storage units, vending machines, or laundromats.

You can self-publish books. This is an example of intellectual property which pays you and your generations forever through royalties.

You can buy a business.

Aside from these pure assets, you can start a variety of businesses.

You can start a lawn-care, cleaning, hair-care, or other business.

You can start an online store like on Amazon, Walmart etc.

You start a business where you "flip" Real Estate, or utilize one of many, many real estate business models.

You can join an MLM (Multi-Level Marketing or Network Marketing company). This is like buying a business with a very small up-front investment. I don't care what anybody else says, the MLM is one of the best attempts at freeing the indoctrinated prisoners - transferring "employee-minded" people into "business-minded" people. When the employee gives up, they are happy to complain to their fellow employees that it's a pyramid scheme and it "doesn't work." I have news for you; your job is a pyramid scheme. Almost everything on earth is a pyramid.

The community, as I mentioned at the beginning of the book, has made a consensus that the job is an acceptable pyramid, and that MLMs are not. Yet, unlike a job, with most (generally speaking of the concept), every single person has a fair shot at making true success. Granted, you have different personality types, or people who come from big and supportive communities etc who might seem to have more "luck." But in the world of business, your mind must transform out of the employee-mindset which is what got you and keeps you where you are - into the business or entrepreneur mind, where there are no excuses; only problem-solving and learning to love it. Why? Because the payoff is worth it, and you must do it to free your children.

You may say, "I don't know anything about ANY of this." Or "I've never had any interest in business." Trust me, this was me. However, the more I learned, the more I realized that all this asset and business stuff wasn't a matter of interest or not interest. Just like a job for most of us, it's a matter of survival. You're going to work anyway. Why not shift your effort towards first LEARNING, and then DOING to get one of these things up and running. You will trip up and fail. Many give up in this process and just return to the safety of the job-prison. That's like the homeless man who will go to steal a piece of candy just so he can get the warmth and security of a jail cell rather than being out in the cold. I am by no means making fun of, or belittling the homeless. In fact, when I say, "Get to the main point of your life" instead of being chained by a job-prision, getting out there and serving the homeless among others, is what I think we could be doing if we weren't so beat down just trying to survive.

Keep trying. It's all going to be work anyway. Whether it's at your job, which is an asset for someone else and their children, or it's going to be you striving to build your own, it will be work.

The difference is in the pay off. It's freedom; financial freedom and freedom from the chains; the bills, the debt, the uncertainty.

There are courses and mentors who are all over the internet who can teach you many of these things. There might be many years of searching, trying this or that. I believe they all work. You just have to work it, or find the thing that works for you. Then, when you have enough money, pay someone to do the business that you know works, but you couldn't do yourself for one reason or the other.

Did you know that Zuckerberg, Gates and about 700 other billionaires did not graduate or go to college, according to a Forbes article? They escaped the prison.

One thing that I will note is that if you start a business, keep it your main aim to acquire true assets. Your lawn care business, for example, only makes money when you work. You want to aim towards either selling your business, or growing it to such a point that it is managed and operated by other (employees) while it simply pays you. After that, you invest (buy) other assets and continue the cycle.

Structures to protect them

In the course of acquiring assets and or business(es), you will invariably discover that there are ways, and in fact by their very nature, businesses must be set up in such a way that they are not under your personal name. This provides ways of significantly lowering your taxes, protecting your money from litigation (being sued), creditors, and other things.

There are things called trusts which are like big containers which can hold your businesses, money, assets, or houses etc which also provide protection both in life and death.

You will learn that you can have a business whose sole reason for existing is to contain your other businesses. It is called a holding company. That holding company can be held by a trust.

You will find there are vast pools of money that are available to these entities that you could not access while you were simply Joe Schmoe the employee. With these, you can acquire even more assets. The money that you make, and the MIND that helped bring you along in this journey has created a social circle of like-minded people who have also have multiple businesses and large net-worths. This is yet another pool of money as these people often partner or joint-venture together in much bigger projects than either of them could have afforded by themselves.

Pass The Wealth Down

From the beginning of your journey, you have already begun passing on the wealth to the next generation. Children learn much more from seeing what you do than from hearing what you say. When this journey gets to its tough spots - of which there are many - keep them in mind. Your input (GIGO) will also be part of that wealth as they hear the podcast, talks, speeches, audio books, and seminars that you're listening to. As you learn about how money works, you will start to guide them better about how they earn money, and what they do with it. Having learnt about compound interest, for instance, you will ensure that they are starting very early in life to invest a moderate amount that will amount to millions by the time that they are 60 years old.

You will learn about starting insurance policies for them which come at their cheapest the younger a person is, that you can pass ownership to them when they become of age or they begin earning enough to pay the premiums themselves.

You will learn how insurance on your own life gives them your money that is protected from creditors, probate , and even some wills.

By having assets, your children never have to go into debt for school (if they insist on school), homes, vacations etc. But in order for them to not blow your hard work within a few years, it is imperative that you train them in everything that you would have learned.

10

CONCLUSION

As I have mentioned about twenty times in this book, this was an overview, a very generalized overview. If you're in business, nothing that I said here is new to you. The cover should have given that away. But this has been for the one to whom the cover is kind of a provocative statement. If you saw the cover and really didn't have an idea - maybe it immediately resonated with you because you already FEEL this way in your bones, but you just want to know "what does he mean?" or "Yes! I want to know where to begin to do better for myself and my kids than this current situation of mine that has me trapped." If this was you when you saw the cover, then this was for you.

But this is just the beginning. As I mentioned, read Rich Dad, Poor Dad, and other books that I will recommend here or in later editions.

The life that most of us live; the "rat race," or the "hamster wheel" or whatever way you've heard it described, you know it, you know the feeling, the reality; that it's a trap! You're a full-grown human, at the peak of your abilities as an adult, but you and BILLIONS of others are willing indentured servants who don't buck the system. We accept and live this barely-alive existence with the utmost docility, and our kids are well on their way to doing the same.

CONCLUSION

Meanwhile, you can SEE that there is different. Others are living it. But how? Sure, some were born into it, but others came from blue-collar homes like yours. Yet now, they work to live, and don't live to work. They earn very well for it, but aren't taxed nearly as much as you are. They seem much more fulfilled and they seem to have more smiles on their faces because while you slave away, they are on golf-courses and open-patio cafes in the middle of the day.

You've been programmed to be this way. Your whole surroundings maintain this invisible prison. Your TV, your family, your community, your schools, and even the courts, the IRS and other government bureaucracies maintain it. You feel like you can't escape it. You have a general sense that it's not right and unfair, but there seems to be no out. It's just the way things are.

But, life is supposed to be for living. If you really want to know, it's for serving God, and then serving others. We're supposed to work, yes, but with enough left over to give to our spouses, children, and communities. We should be able to retire at a not-too-old age, with enough time left to rest, serve others, and enjoy our families and neighbors.

That's why when we work, we should work with the aim of being able to stop HAVING to work way before retirement age, and then being able to pass on something significant to our children, and their children.

Those who are free live with this mindset. It takes time and effort and changing one's input and surroundings, but it is doable. With this mindset, money is meant to work for you. It is supposed to eventually buy more assets which will then make even more money for you.

You can learn how insurance, trusts, and business structures can work in your favor to protect your money and ensure that the bulk of it passes to your children instead of disappearing through taxes and probate (a long process that finds every one who must be paid from your life first [if there's no will] before your kids can access it. This can take years and eat into your inheritance with lawyer fees and other costs).

Perhaps in future I will expound on the ideas in this book, perhaps with some topics having their own books. But my goal is to eventually put out into the world information to bring someone from where I was in my financial (il)literacy to a point of freedom; maybe even with specific business courses that explain step by step how to start; from beginner, to intermediate, and to advanced in terms of the money and the knowledge that they have to get started. I want to help someone even if they are starting from tens of thousands of dollars in debt, to create a real income that isn't just pennies, or if it is, that those pennies are completely passive, so that all they have to do is duplicate until those pennies become dollars, then hundreds, then thousands. And then they can get themselves ASSETS.

Final note: I'm practicing what I'm preaching. This will be an ASSET for my family and I, by God's grace. Therefore:

If you found this book helpful, I'd be very appreciative if you left a positive review for the book on Amazon and then share with others!

Thanks

11

RESOURCES

Wachowski, Brothers. (Director). (1999). *The Matrix* [Film]. by: Warner Bros., Roadshow Entertainment.

Blend. (2022, November 8). *Origin Stories: The meaning of mortgage*. Blend. https://blend.com/blog/thought-leadership/origin-stories-mortgage/

Owens, R., Orwell, G., Hall, W. E., & Miles, W. A. (1963). *George Orwell's 1984: A Play in Three Acts*. Dramatic Publishing.

Kiyosaki, R. T. (2009). *Rich dad, poor dad: What the rich teach their kids about Money—That the poor and the middle class do not!* http://ci.nii.ac.jp/ncid/BA50082780

Murray, C. (2022, October 15). These are the richest Americans who never went to college. *Forbes*. https://www.forbes.com/sites/conormurray/2022/10/15/these-are-the-richest-americans-who-never-went-to-college/?sh=462b869d6097

Kagan, J. (2024, May 15). *Probate: what it is and how it works with and without a will*. Investopedia. https://www.investopedia.com/terms/p/probate.asp#toc-probate-without-a-will

www.ingramcontent.com/pod-product-compliance
Lightning Source LLC
Chambersburg PA
CBHW050249230526
45470CB00005B/2177